ABC of the Web™

Alphabet primer
for young developers
in training

<!-- a code babies book -->

For Baby Gray and Little Jack

Alphabet primer for young developers in training

<!-- a code babies book -->

A  is for **Anchor tag**

Code an A

Download an A

What begins with A?

Anchor tag brings elements together for a day

B

is for **Browser**

Blog a B

Backlog a B

What begins with B?

Browser looks for
keywords on the
internet tree

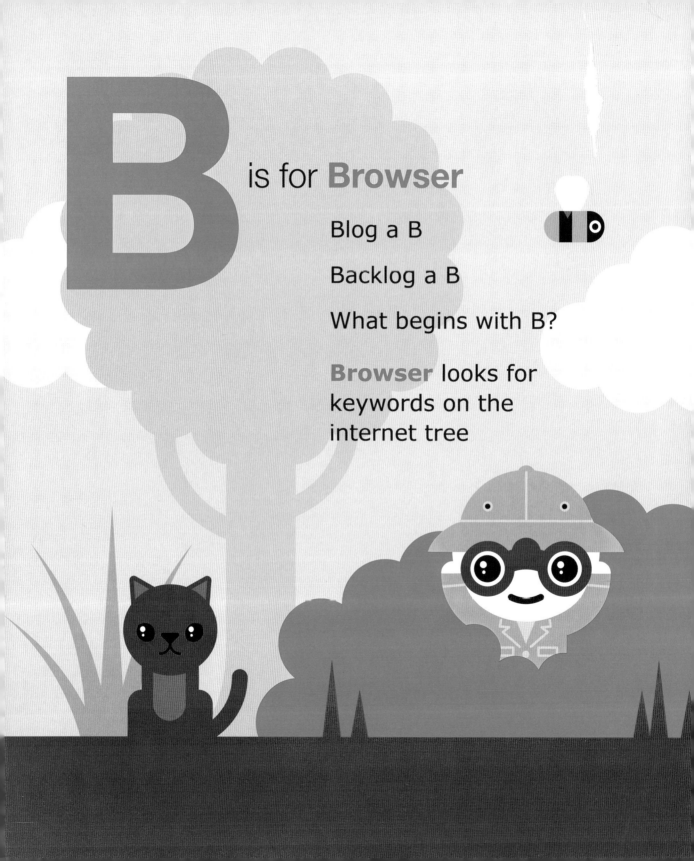

 is for **Cookie**

Fade a C

Cascade a C

What begins with C?

Cookies store your page views, and keep your privacy

Keep Off!

COOKIES

D
is for
Domain

Array a D

Display a D

What begins with D?

Domains are
special places for
web pages to be

E

is for Elements

Script an E

Zip an E

What begins with E?

Elements are building
blocks for websites
that you see

F is for **Function**

Style an F

Rasterize an F

What begins with F?

Functions have specific tasks like zoom, delete, or half

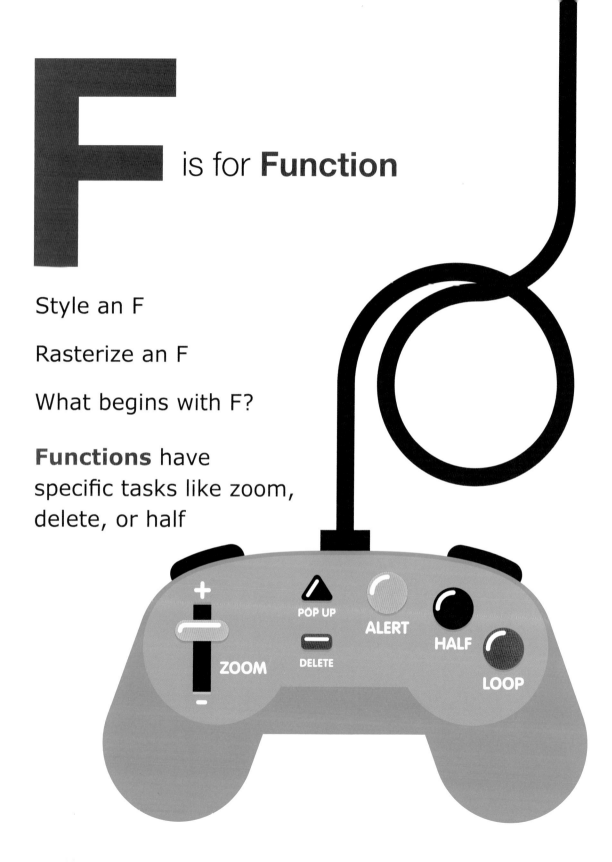

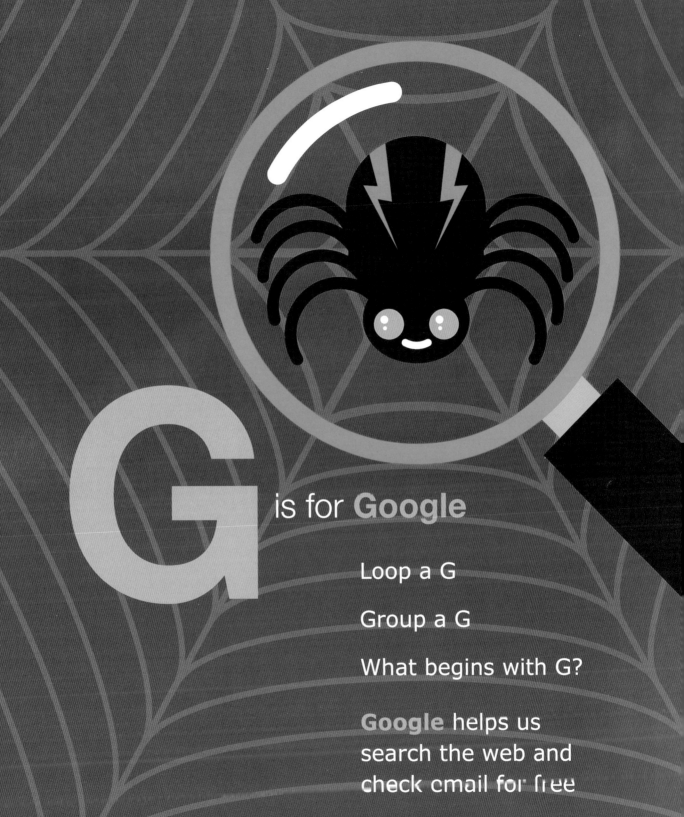

G

is for **Google**

Loop a G

Group a G

What begins with G?

Google helps us
search the web and
check email for free

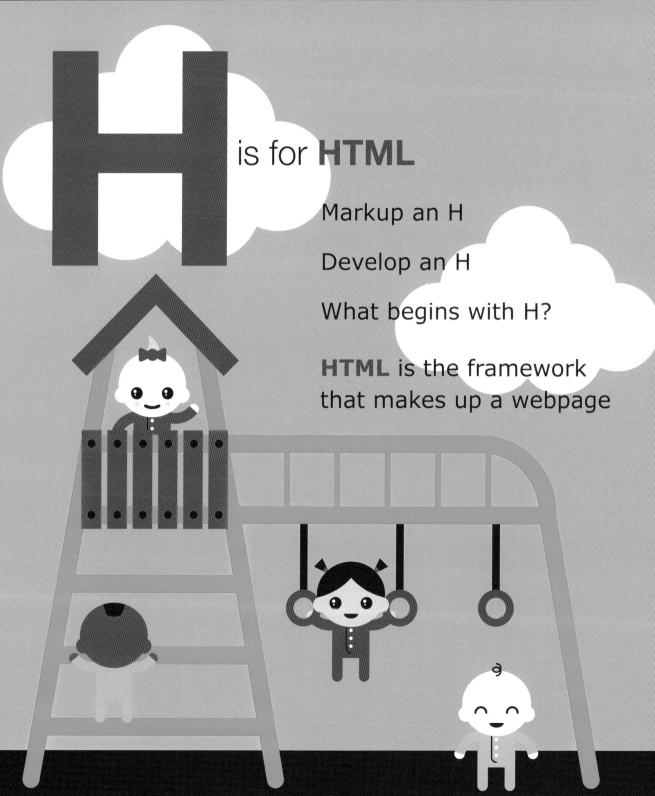

H is for **HTML**

Markup an H

Develop an H

What begins with H?

HTML is the framework that makes up a webpage

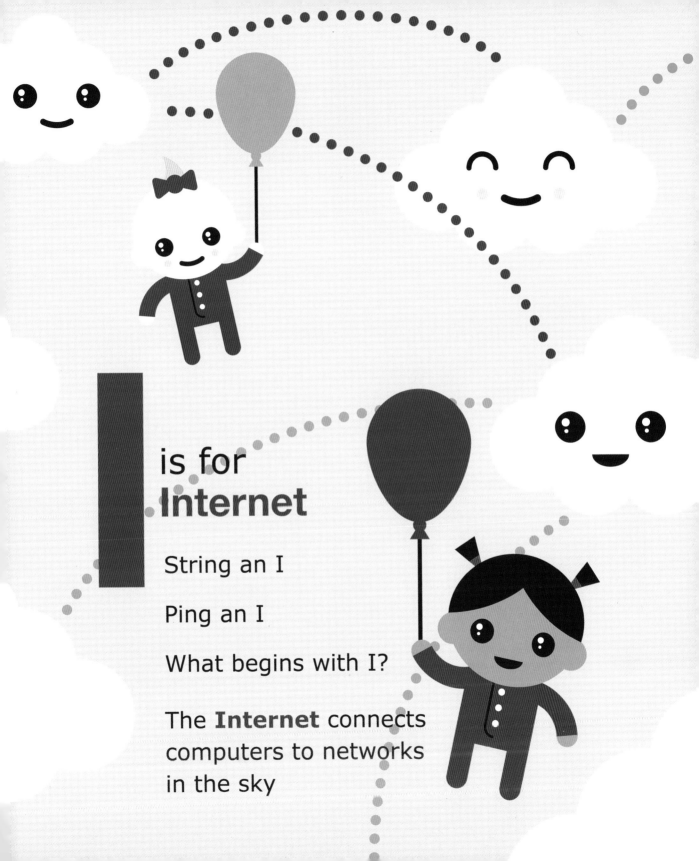

I is for Internet

String an I

Ping an I

What begins with I?

The **Internet** connects computers to networks in the sky

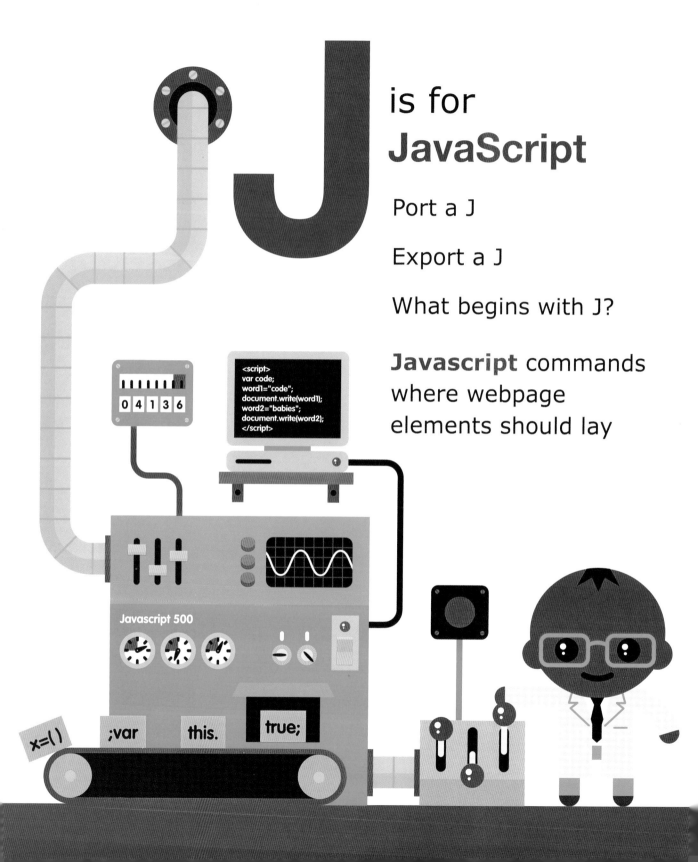

J is for **JavaScript**

Port a J

Export a J

What begins with J?

Javascript commands where webpage elements should lay

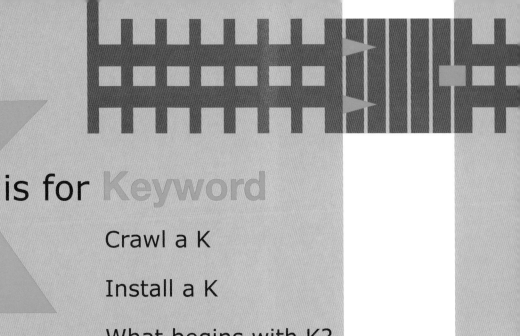

K is for Keyword

Crawl a K

Install a K

What begins with K?

Keywords guide
browsers and help
them find their way

PARK ▼

◄ WOODS

L is for Link

Slide an L

Align an L

What begins with L?

Links are shortcuts between pages so you don't have to dwell

M is for Mozilla

Animate an M

Navigate an M

What begins with M?

Mozilla makes
non-profit and
open-source programs

N

is for **Node.js**

Hack an N

Unpack an N

What begins with N?

Node.js is code
that does more tricks
than most stunt men

O is for Open Source

Click an O

Transmit an O

What begins with O?

Open source is sharing
code and adding what
you know

P is for **PHP**

Host a P

Post a P

What begins with P?

PHP helps websites
and databases agree

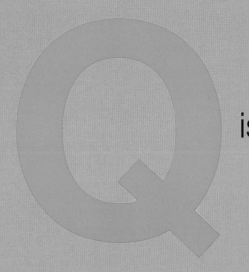

Q is for Query

Float a Q

Quote a Q

What begins with Q?

Queries can ask
a website specific
things to do

R  is for **Ruby**

Transport an R

Support an R

What begins with R?

Ruby is a full-stack code that makes sites look like stars

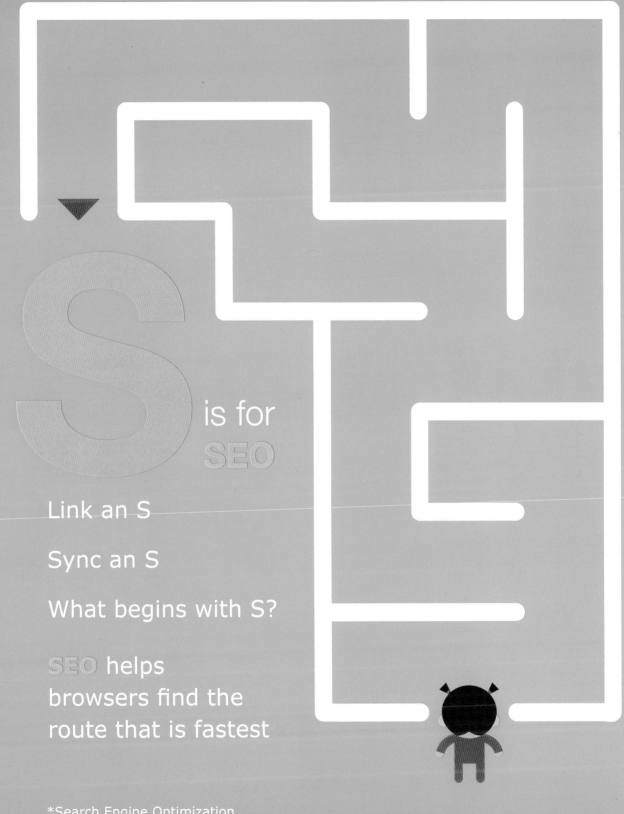

S is for SEO

Link an S

Sync an S

What begins with S?

SEO helps browsers find the route that is fastest

*Search Engine Optimization

T is for **Tag**

Nest a T

Test a T

What begins with T?

Tags indicate what style webpage elements should be

The Codebabies
4 Internet Street
World Wide Web
CB
01010

46

U

is for **URL**

Select a U

Connect a U

What begins with U?

URL is a web
address that browsers
can come to

*Uniform Resource Locator

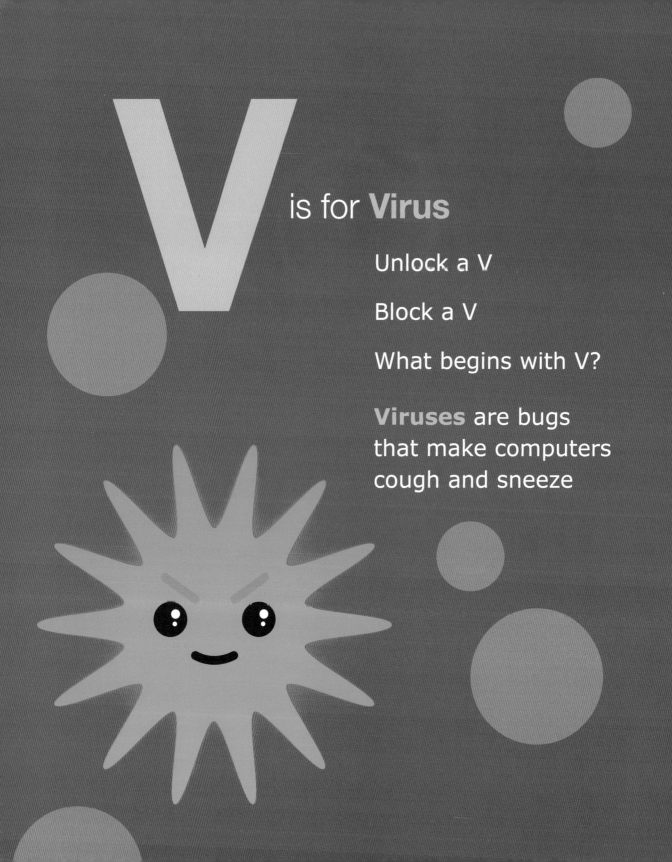

V is for **Virus**

Unlock a V

Block a V

What begins with V?

Viruses are bugs that make computers cough and sneeze

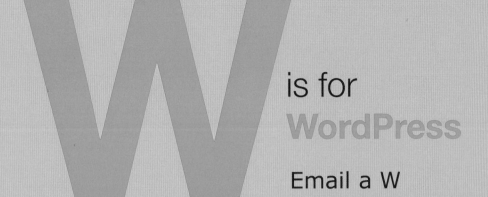

W is for WordPress

Email a W

Scale a W

What begins with W?

Wordpress is a blog
program to help relay
the news

X is for XML

Store an X

Explore an X

What begins with X?

XML lets users
speaking differently
connect

Voice
Changer

*Extensible Markup Language

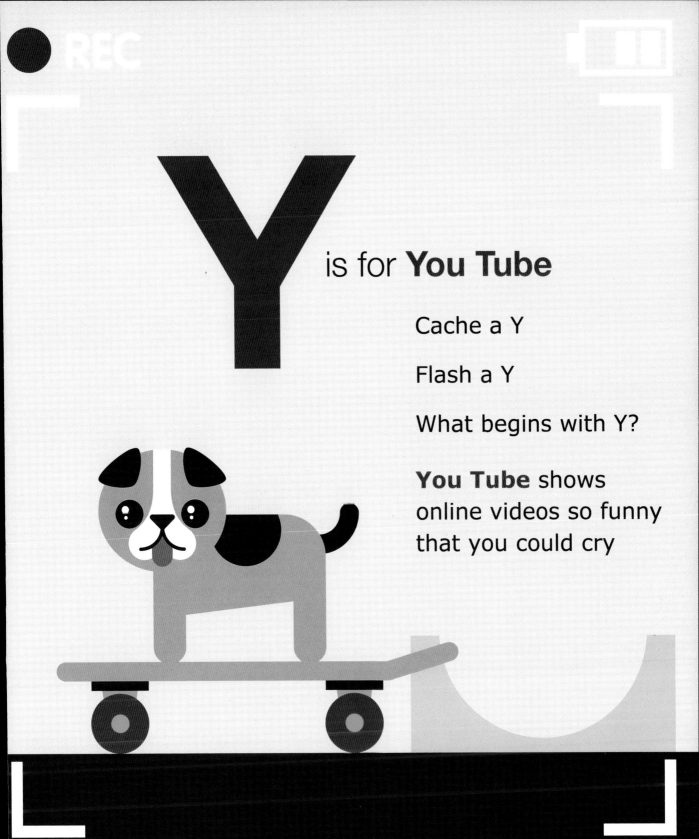

REC

Y

is for **You Tube**

Cache a Y

Flash a Y

What begins with Y?

You Tube shows online videos so funny that you could cry

Z

is for **Z-index**

Route a Z

Checkout a Z

What begins with Z?

Z-index is the order in which elements should be

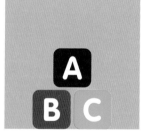

We would love to hear from you!
Let us know what you think
or just say hi :-) at:

codebabies.com
Facebook.com/CodeBabiesBooks
Twitter: @codebabies

Also by Code Babies

Find them on codebabies.com
or ask for them at your
local bookstore